CRANGLEGATE

A MEMOIR OF LONDON TO THE COUNTRY

ROSALIND BUCKIE

For my dear family and friends

CONTENTS

ISBN 978-1-913584-13-9 hardback

ISBN 978-1-913584-14-6 paperback

Written and illustrated by Rosalind Buckie

First published in Great Britain in 2022 by Leopard Print

FOREWORD

BY NIGEL BUCKIE

In a strange turn of events one bright and sunny morning, I received a telephone call from my mother.

'Oh, and I have written a book,' she said.

'What?' I said.

'Yes,' she said, 'I told you.'

'No, you didn't.'

That was the start, and after receiving what looked like a school exercise notebook through the post labelled *Cranglegate*, the adventure began.

Cranglegate was the name of the house that we had moved to from our beloved London. I was the youngest. I was 9. My brother and

BY NIGEL BUCKIE

I really did think our parents had gone a little mad, and a little off the beaten path for sure — to the wild and woolly depths of the countryside. Where exactly was it where we'd found ourselves?

Back then the roads weren't so good and Norfolk was much more remote to get to. We later realised many people in Norfolk had never been to London and were quite suspicious of us.

I always remember getting to the house and thinking, *surely this isn't where we are moving to?* It looked like it hadn't been lived in for years. The front was all overgrown and you couldn't even get in the front door. My immediate thought was, 'Why have they brought us all the way up here? Are they going to leave us here and drive back to London?' I could see that same thought on my older brother's face, the look of disbelief.

Of course it wasn't long before we were let loose and exploring the house and garden which we loved. However it was a bit different at night when there was no power and therefore no lights, but more of that later in my mother's own words. Also, for us, going to a new school in the country was, well, an "education", let's just say that.

The Saturday market was full of live-stock auction selling rabbits, ducks and things we had never seen in London. It made for an interesting day, being a busy marketplace which we could also explore.

As time went on we began to enjoy the freedom we had around the town which we certainly never did in London, not to the extent we had then, and to visit the "wreck" as we called it to some of our newfound friends. Perhaps it wasn't so bad after all. I am sure we never realised at the time the impact on my mother or father during that move. To us they had simply gone a tad off the beaten track.

A BRIEF HISTORY OF CRANGLEGATE HOUSE

Historically a coaching inn called the "Maid's Head", the house's main facade seen today was put on in the 17th Century (c.

1740) and so appears to be Georgian but is actually from an earlier period. Nikolaus Pevsner mentions Swaffham and the house. See excerpt from listed building listing below.

The house has many fine Georgian sash windows to the facade with three levels the top one being with the roof with dormer windows. Some of the windows can be seen to have been bricked up due to the window tax at that time. There are a few other fine houses and buildings situated around the market square which in its heyday was an important market town and the houses demonstrated its importance.

A fine historical town, Swaffham has a thriving Saturday market square with many stalls and "live" livestock auction of goats, sheep, cows, rabbits and chickens, and up to 22 pubs around the market place to help keep the lively atmosphere going all day and into the night.

Swaffham is also known for "The Pedlar of Swaffham" whose story says he found a pot of gold on his way to London after having a dream about it, which funded the building of Swaffham Church.

Later, Swaffham was home to Howard Carter who discovered Tutankhamen's tomb and hence there is a Museum in the square dedicated to him and his finds with Lord Carnarvon in Cairo, Egypt. Harry Carter also carved many of Norfolk's fine village and town signs and Swaffham's sign depicts the Swaffham Pedlar's story.

The Maid's Head Inn, as it was originally known, would have been a main stop-off point for people travelling from the town and from the North Norfolk coast to London and elsewhere. Lord Nelson reportedly stayed at the Inn on his way from his home in Burnham Thorpe to London and when travelling back.

The house has a fine staircase and entrance hallway with an encaustic tiled floor leading through to the rear and the original 16ft curing ceiling of the kitchen and original scullery space.

There are two wells: one in the garden near the old coach house and another in the cellar to provide spring water for the house.

The cellar is said to have a tunnel to the church across the road and to the market square. There were also a couple of priest holds hidden within the house to harbour priests during the persecution of Catholics.

The house boasts the original panelled window shutters and gun racks in the hallway leading to the kitchen. The hallway near the rear garden door often had rabbits and pheasants hanging outside the kitchen.

ARCHITECTURAL HISTORY

From listed building listing:
SWAFFHAM

TF8109 MARKET PLACE 809-1/5/68 (North side) 10/01/51 No.59 Cranglegate GV II

House. c1740. Red brick; roof of black-glazed pantiles. EXTERIOR: 2 storeys and dormer attic. 9-window range, the window to left on each floor blind. Central 6- panelled and fielded door under a 6-vaned fanlight. Panelled reveals. Doorcase with block entablatures supporting open segmental pediment. Fenestration of 6/6 unhorned sashes, those to ground floor under gauged skewback arches, to first floor with gauged segmental arches. Platband at first floor. Saw-toothed eaves cornice. Gabled roof. 4 flat-topped dormers fitted with 3/3 horned sashes (that to right without horns). Internal gable-end stack to west. Single-storey bay attached to east return with a half-glazed door. Rear elevation with 2 stacks on wall plane, and a 2-storey extension.

INTERIOR: not inspected but likely to be of interest.

Historical and architectural notes by:
Nigel Buckie

CRANGLEGATE

Fig. 1. Cranglegate. Pencil and watercolour on paper

INTRODUCTION

This book is about Keith and I, our two boys Andrew and Nigel, and Brumas, our Old English sheepdog, taking on an empty Grade II-listed building.

It was Keith's dream to have an antique shop with good accommodation for the family. It became a tremendous challenge and not for the faint-hearted as you will see.

Hopefully you will enjoy and appreciate our story.

Rosalind Buckie

CHAPTER 1

MOVING IN

CRANGLEGATE

12th February 1973

I SHOULD HAVE WRITTEN THIS YEARS AGO BUT I will just jot down what I and maybe others can remember. I know it was a cold start for it was winter.

Our old London house was empty as the removal men had been. Keith's younger brother, Tony, had bought the house from us. The bit that was most vivid was when Tony came round with his friend Kevin. I was trying to zip Nigel up in his anorak but couldn't get it to work through the tears. Kevin kindly stepped in and sorted it for me whilst Tony just waltzed upstairs. We said our goodbyes and started the long journey to Norfolk. I suppose we must have stopped somewhere to eat en route but it was a long emotional drive.

WE ARRIVED AT THIS GORGEOUS, overgrown, empty large house that was cold and unloved and dirty. The boys could not believe it. Why have we left a comfortable finished house for this? I think we were asking ourselves the same question.

Our dear friend Douglas had come with Keith a week ago to bring garden stuff and had made up two beds pushed together in the front room on the left of the front door. We had brought bedding with us so it was aired. The kitchen was tiny and the cooker filthy. Oh, I must have been mad to agree to this. Keith had put my old sewing table and the garden pub table in the kitchen so we could eat there. The only heat was from big storage heaters which were ugly and useless.

WE MUST HAVE EATEN and then we all piled into bed, Keith and I at one end, and Andrew and Nigel at the other end. The boys and I got the giggles; mine were more like hysteria. It was cold and noisy from the traffic for we were on the main crossroads. Keith got mad, and we all ended up crying. What have we done? He wanted a house and shop combined but we hadn't even got planning permission yet after seven months.

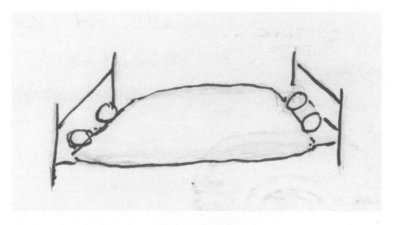

Fig. 2. The bed

~

THE NEXT MORNING after a fitful sleep we rose. I was trying to find breakfast stuff for us whilst the boys explored and chose their rooms. Fortunately, Andrew chose the small room next to the bathroom, so Nigel was able to have a large bedroom for all his hobbies. Keith just walked around like a zombie, fazed out by what he had done and where he'd brought us to.

There was a knock on the door. The removal men were here.

'You'll have to clear this, mate, because we can't get past this lot,' one of them said, referring to the overgrown hedges. Keith went to find the cutters that he had brought with him in the garden stuff and started chopping.

Then so many questions like 'where do you want this?' and 'where should we put this?' followed. We roughly sorted what went where to be sorted later.

The boys had found the room opposite the big kitchen which we had a lot of junk in left by the previous owners. They were busy sorting through that and it kept them occupied.

Fig. 3 - Front door of Cranglegate

WE HAD BOUGHT the house from a wildlife photographer who had literally camped in it for the last couple of years. The plan was for his parents to move in to look after it for him but they finally declined. He decided to sell it to us after we saw it on a previous visit to the town to look at another property. Keith put a note through the door saying, 'if you ever want to sell, I'm interested'.

He'd said that it was a beautiful house lending itself to a combined shop/house with a garden for the boys and dog, and a garage.

However, it was very old house.

THE GEORGIAN FAÇADE was put on in the 1760s, and luckily, the staircase and alcoves too. We later learnt that it had been a coaching inn called "The Maids Head" prior to the 1700s and after that the house had been in the hands of many surgeons and doctors. Indeed the doctor's surgery would become our shop as there was an end door for the patients to come in!

Keith had it all worked out but hadn't quite realised the work it would take or the amount of time and money.

My job at first was to make it clean and

to make it a home. It was so cold that I wore many woollen clothes to keep myself warm even though I was working. I tackled the bedrooms and drawing room first. Then I sorted the boiler room as it was especially horrid with a filthy stove.

I MUST HAVE BEEN mad to agree to this. I loved the beauty of the house but it was too much and too far away from all I knew and loved. Most of our stuff fitted in but the boys had wardrobes that Douglas had made which were too tall.

He was coming up to stay when we got another bed, to saw the wardrobes in half and reduce them.

THE DRAWING ROOM was made fairly comfortable even though wallpaper was hanging off in places and the beautiful alcoves were painted the most horrible "babies' yellow".

We all huddled here at night in front of the blazing fire using wood found from around the garden and the dilapidated sheds.

We used to toss a coin and pluck up the courage for who was going to make a night time drink. It seemed like going down to the dungeons. It was all so dark and gloomy, and so far away from the rest of the family.

A lot of boxes remained packed as there was nowhere to put the stuff. There were no kitchen cupboards so the boxes were left in the big kitchen, which we rifled through when we needed something.

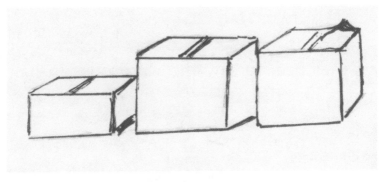

Fig. 4 - The boxes

CHAPTER 2

HEATING

OF COURSE, THE SECOND WEEK OF BEING there, it snowed. It was so bitterly cold.

How did we survive?

We were young, I suppose.

The boys couldn't believe what we had done though they were excited about the house too.

We realised that we must put central heating in first and sort the shop area to make it presentable. The planning approval came in two months after being here.

MR MATSELL WAS the chap we chose to put in the heating. His assessor advised too many radiators which Keith argued against, being difficult to place furniture.

We certainly didn't need one in the boiler room. The boiler to go in was a mini-industrial one to cope with the size and many changing floor levels of the house.

The heating engineers were supposed to be there for six weeks but stretched it to be much longer, to March and April. Fortunately the weather was fine so I escaped to the garden when I could to plan and decorate the rooms. We had managed to tame the garden a bit. It was looking pretty but still wild with daffodils.

KEITH HAD PULLED down numerous sheds and some weird sort of cage used for fruit or wild animals.

A lot of the ground was cleared and we needed a new vehicle entrance as the council decided the one we and others before us used was too near the junction. They would not let us come across the alley as we have to cross the butcher's right-of-way. We

ended up at the far end of the garden, the
only place, really.

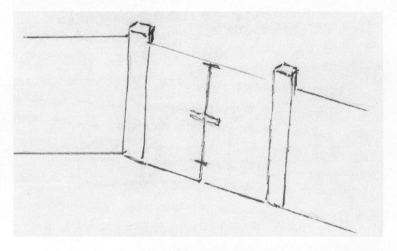

Fig. 5. The main gates

CHAPTER 3

SCHOOL

BY THIS TIME I HAD INTRODUCED THE BOYS to their new school. The other children thought they were from another planet, what with the long hair and coming from London which seemed so far away in those days.

Both of them were exceedingly good-looking so the girls loved them, even chasing them home. They thought I was their sister as I wore my Dr Zhivago long black coat with toggle fastenings and fur-edged hood and cuffs.

It was the only coat that kept me warm. It got me not another glance in London but was a bit exotic here back then.

Fig. 6 - Me in my black coat

~

THE SCHOOL always contributed to Carnival Day which was always held in the Summer, in which Sue Polaine, a teacher, was always very active. She also ran the Charity here for World Wildlife Fund.

One year she had a float on this theme.

Andrew was to sit on a nest wearing an "eagle's head". Keith made a marvellous looking head which we fixed onto a sort of scarf or snood so it tied under his chin, keeping it on. I also made a "tiger's skin" out of an old blanket, stuffing the head which was draped over the school gym horse. Other parents had turned their children into all sorts of animals.

TWO THINGS WERE against this being the great success it should have been. Sue was let down on the size of the trailer lorry. The one that turned up was far too small to give the display justice.

It also turned out to be the hottest day of the year. Andrew nearly fainted with the heat. We had to buy an ice lolly to stick on his head.

He was very glad to get off.

NIGEL ALSO COMPETED ANOTHER YEAR. He was the back end of a horse with his friend Barry Knox.

They had to walk the course and got very wet as it rained. Nigel used to play tennis with Barry and was always Björn Borg with the headband.

Fig. 6a - Andrew as an eagle

Fig. 6b - Nigel as the rear of a pantomime horse

CHAPTER 4

BUILDERS

KEITH WAS HAVING A TUSSLE WITH THE Council over the huge 1 hour-rated fire door from the shop to the house. It meant taking the original Georgian door off and the new one was just plain. They were adamant that as the building was Grade II-listed, we'd had to have a fire-proof door and ceiling tiles. The upstairs drawing room had to be hardboarded and sealed — such a big job taking lots of time and money before we could even think of opening. Keith was to do this as he did many things to save money and to do a proper job. The builders were so busy when we came that we had to resort to finding someone from the local papers. Certain jobs, such as a new roof for what was to become a workshop and store room at the back, and the new vehicle entrance, were part of the mortgage agreement.

"Mr Builder" duly turned up without tools to assess and start the work. Whilst he was a good bricky, he and his mate were haphazard in their work. They went down the pubs at lunchtime, indulging a little too much at times. We had a fire one night where they had dropped a cigarette end onto the timbers they had left on the floor of the workshop. Keith had asked them to remove all the timber as the cellar was underneath.

Oh, that will be all right, they said. They were lazy and careless in so many ways.

I went to the loo one night to find it foggy. I told Keith but he said it was my imagination. Then when he used it later, the fog was thicker. He could then smell the smoke. On going downstairs, he discovered one of the huge beams smouldering. With superhuman effort, he somehow managed to pull it out onto the grass. We poured water over it and the rest. On telling "Mr Builder" and the helper, he feigned surprise at how this could have happened.

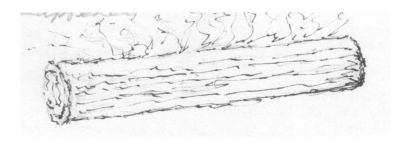

Fig. 7. Smouldering logs

Dropping ends of cigarettes was how it happened.

Another time we were up all night as the rain poured through. Luckily the back hall flowed downwards to the front. We were able to continually "sweep" the water through and out of the front door. This was to keep it out of the kitchen which was lower.

Again, the "builders" wondered how this could have happened. It did because they hadn't covered the roof area as Keith had asked them.

. . .

WE'D HAD six weeks of dry, good weather but we knew that would not last in England. Thankfully, the "builders" did know a good carpenter who renewed all the wooden joists.

Oh, I forgot another issue. When they were taking the roof off, the loo walls fell in so Keith had to sort that out. We had an "open air loo" for a short time. The "builders" did quite a lot of work here over which Keith watched. When asked why he was watching them, he told them so he didn't have to employ them again.

Fig. 8. Me, holding a broom in the hallway

Of course, most of this work, if not all,
was done before the heating was fitted. We

had decided on oil as we had so much trouble with sea gas at the previous house and electric was expensive. The daft thing was that you still had to have electricity to power the pump.

I did manage to clean most of the rooms so at least they were habitable.

CHAPTER 5

MEALS

I HAD SCRUBBED THE BOILER ROOM AND cooker where I made big pots of stew to last a few days. It was soup and a sandwich most days for lunch but we did have some good countryside meals and the following were the basic recipes I used at the time.

BEEF STEW WITH DUMPLINGS

Serves 4-5

For the stew:

You will need:

- Oil for frying
- 2 lbs stewing steak

- 2 onions
- 2 parsnips
- 2 large potatoes
- 2 celery sticks
- 4 carrots
- 4 large mushrooms
- Herbs eg thyme, bay leaves
- 2 beef stock cubes

Method:

1. Cut steak and all vegetables into chunks.
2. Heat oil until hot. Brown steak in oil. Top with water to cover. Add 2 stock cubes and herbs.
3. Bring to the boil then simmer until tender. Add more liquid if necessary.
4. Alternative: Slow cook in a pre-heated oven at 150 deg C for about 2 hours. Serve with cabbage or other green vegetable.

For the dumplings:
You will need:

- 4 oz self-raising flour
- 2 oz shredded suet
- 1 tsp mixed herbs
- Pinch of salt

Method:
Combine the above with enough water to lightly mould into enough balls for family.

Enjoy.

RABBIT AND PHEASANT

I also cooked rabbit and pheasant in this way, usually in the oven slowly after Keith had knocked them over. They were fiddly to skin or pluck the feathers.

Cut the game into portions enough for the family, adding chunks of eating apple and using chicken stock with similar vegetables.

Fig. 9. My countryside stews

Fig. 10. Vegetables on our kitchen table

CHAPTER 6

CHRISTMAS

I REMEMBER ONE DAY WHEN KEITH AND I had a row over something. He stormed off just before lunch. I was waiting for ages. I ended up eating on my own. When he came in he said he had eaten at the little cafe a few doors away.

I was livid.

HE'D BROUGHT me so far away from everyone I knew because of what he wanted. To be treated like that when I had worked as best as I could cleaning and cooking and making a home. I was out of there if he did that again.

I just wanted a good life for me, him and the boys.

THINGS WERE FROSTY FOR A WHILE. The cold, dirt, emptiness and loneliness were getting me down.

I did manage to phone Hazel a few times but mum wasn't on the phone then though my sister Nessa was. We compared the weather and caught up with their news. We got through the summer and opened the shop in October 1973. The press came to do a little write up and take photos. I never liked the photo though.

WE RAN the shop together but mostly Keith was in there at first except when he was buying or renovating something, that was mostly furniture or the house. He also attended local auctions and had certain private calls.

Most of the time in those early days he went back to London to buy at his old haunts, calling in at Baldock on the way home on a couple of good antique dealers shops there.

It was always exciting to see what he had got. Sometimes he would visit his parents, staying a long time to chat, and occasionally buying some pieces from his father who had built up quite a collection which he had a job to house. He was always hard to deal with as he didn't really like Keith selling them on, but that was how we earned our living.

CHRISTMAS

We got through Christmas mostly with the boys and I playing games whilst Keith's head was stuck in a book. It was a mistake to give him a book for Christmas as that's where his focus would be.

Fig. 11. Picture of chair and us playing games

CHAPTER 7

UPHEAVAL

THE NEWS WASN'T GOOD IN THE NEW YEAR with a lot of unrest. This was especially so with the miners.

They wanted more wages and better working conditions, and so went on strike to get them. Who could blame them? What a horrid way to earn a living but necessary for us all to keep warm and powered.

The police were out in force and it all got very nasty for quite a while. Finally, they capitulated as they were suffering and had families to keep. Margaret Thatcher wasn't giving way. I do think she was wrong on this though the thought was other

Unions would climb onto the bandwagon because they were strong then.

We ended up with a 'three day week' and lots of power cuts. I remember us lighting the shop with tilly lamps. I deemed it a good day if I managed to sell something under those circumstances. It was very hard. And it was extremely miserable. On those days I would often help the boys with their homework huddled around the fire in the drawing room.

KEITH SAW an advert for trading at a London market so decided to have a look.

Oh, no! We'd moved here to end up doing a market in London but that's where the trade was. We did it for many years as it saved our bacon.

It was a long day, getting up very early to travel down where the buzz of early dealers would be.

LATER ON THE people from outside the area would come and then still later, the tourists.

So we had quite a few shots at selling our wares.

We met some lovely people too from all walks of life trading in all sorts of different stock— dealers with shops like us, actors and lecturers supplementing their income and even some from stately homes. Some of them became firm friends for many years.

Mind you, it was very tiring. We would stop on the way home at the edge of Epping Forest for a 20-minute nap, and have coffee and a sandwich before setting off again.

GOT a rude awakening after one particular rest as the car was being bumped about.

I opened my eyes to see a cow staring in at me. Thankfully, she soon moved off when she saw me — such a big animal with very long lashes to die for. Cows grazed there before the leader would take them safely across the busy main road.

CHAPTER 8

KEITH'S FRIENDS

ONE TIME KEITH'S FRIEND, SYLVIA Thornton, brought John Le Mesurier to visit. She was the makeup artist on the *Dad's Army* television series which they were filming at Thetford. She wasn't happy when she arrived as she had backed into a petrol pump in a local garage and damaged the car.

They sat on the sofa in the drawing room where I served them tea. John was very quiet but surprised us all by saying what a lovely room it was, which it was, apart from the wallpaper falling off behind him and yucky painted alcoves. He was right, though. It was lovely, a life-saver that would be most attractive when finally decorated to our taste.

KEITH HAD MET Sylvia at his miniaturist art class run by Mrs Court. I also became friendly with Sylvia and her family who were all slightly eccentric but very talented. When I was 21 she came to the flat with a bottle of perfume which cheered me up immediately as I was on my own with Andrew as a baby. She later informed me that her sister had chicken pox. Oh dear. I was worried then because although I'd had it, Andrew hadn't. I went to the doctor after she had left. He assured me that babies under 3 months were immune so that reassured me.

It was very sweet and thoughtful of her. She also cut and styled my hair a few times. Her sister was in the fashion business, her mother made wonderful lampshades and her father became a very talented artist in his retirement.

· · ·

KEITH WAS Mrs Court's protégé so was not pleased when I came on the scene but soon realised that I would not interfere. He was very successful in the late 50s and early 60s. He exhibited in the Royal Academy, the Royal Portrait Society, The Royal Water-colour Society and The Paris Salon. Keith soon realised that people would not pay for a small painted portrait so it went by the board when Mrs Court died and our family took priority.

13th September 2020

YES, quite a jump, but it is Keith's 80th birthday. It is a Sunday and a beautiful day spent with the family except the boys' lady friends!

We got it in just before 'the rule of six' because of the horrendous Covid-19 pandemic.

I asked the boys what they remembered of their first day here. They said, 'Sleeping or trying to in that awful bed, top to tail

plus having to come in the back way because the bushes so overgrown we couldn't
get in the front door!'

I hadn't remembered the latter. I suppose I was so glad we had arrived.

CHAPTER 9

SHOP

I PAPERED THE HALLWAY AND THE STAIRS IN A traditional dark pink pattern with Keith's help. This is never to be repeated as it was so difficult. I remembered one very slow day in the shop when we had furniture across the hallway in what was the dining room. A couple came through saying how they loved the wallpaper. I felt like doing a "John Cleese" and ripping it off to give it to them! Of all the stock we had, they preferred the wallpaper.

Another couple came in to play out a TV programme game where you had to guess what each other liked. I informed them we were just about to close for half an hour to grab some lunch but if they were serious they could come back afterwards.

This was not a game but a business in which we made our living. They did come back apologising, assuring me they were serious. They were local vets and busy furnishing their home. I am pleased to say they became good customers and a pleasure to serve. Another time I had a very strange chap in, but where was Keith?

I had to cajole him along and listen to his woes. It seemed he had broken up with his wife over her domineering ways. Fortune and patience paid off for he ended up spending something. Thank goodness for my perseverance. We earned money.

I DID OFTEN FEEL like a social worker or a place for lonely hearts. I was also a travel bureau for people visiting the area who would often ask for the best places to visit.

It was also a meeting place especially on a Saturday — market day.

Fortunately these people often bought

presents for their friends or themselves as a reminder of their trip to Norfolk.

IN THOSE EARLY DAYS, furniture was a great selling point. We would often get other dealers in the week buying to resell in their own establishments, and individuals from all walks of life because they loved what we had. They could also say that they'd bought it from that nice antique shop on the corner in Swaffham opposite the George Hotel. We did advertise a lot in those early days in the Norfolk magazine and EDP.

THE REST of the shops here benefitted too as that was another reason we came to Swaffham. There were several other antique and picture galleries in the town all carrying a high standard of stock.

Mrs Carter had a great place where the Woods Gun Shop is now. The Troman's Gallery was around the corner with paintings, etchings and so on. Then up the High Street there was Hayes Gallery with mostly antique paintings. Across the road was Blaines, Mr and Mrs White and further up, Ralph Cross. Alan Cole was in Lynn Road where the Horse and Groom is now. This was the place that brought us to Swaffham one very snowy day.

Andrew Blaine had it but when we arrived he informed us it was under offer but might not go through. It did. I was pleased as it was much colder that end of town. That was when we spotted Cranglegate. We did become very friendly with Alan and his family. He was a very clever artist but dealt in country stuff. We did buy from different dealers here and always sent people round to them all. This was not always reciprocated.

I WAS LEFT MORE and more to sell in the shop while Keith renovated stock, the house and went on buying trips. I remember Saturdays being particularly busy with people hanging on to items they wished to buy in case someone else picked them up.

We still had the furniture room across

the hallway open but only put decorative items in the window and to decorate certain pieces.

ONE SATURDAY we had a group of Americans come in who were staying at the George Hotel. It wasn't until later that we discovered a pair of large candlesticks and decanters were missing. They had kept us busy in the silver cabinets whilst they walked out the front door with them. We called the police telling them of our suspicions, asking them to send plain clothes people. A "bobby" arrived in a very noticeable "uniform" but he did go over to the Hotel where they were staying and then came back to say all cases were sealed, ready for customs.

Even the hotel staff had their suspicions, but that was that, as far as the police were concerned. They later discovered that those Americans had committed similar crimes throughout Norfolk and Suffolk but we never got our goods back or compensation.

· · ·

GENERALLY, people were honest and a pleasure to deal with but not long after, we closed that room. It was difficult to keep an eye on. We did keep some pieces in there that we let certain dealers look at and it was handy if Keith wanted to do private transactions. Mainly, it was turned into our dining room.

We still had to keep a watch on people as certain ones like to put things in their pockets. I had to remind them that those items needed to be paid for.

ONE LATE SATURDAY, I had a couple of gypsy boys come in under the pretence that they wanted to buy their mother something for Mother's Day. They kept splitting up to make it difficult for me to watch them but I knew they were out to pilfer. Finally one left and I suggested to the older one it might be best if he brought in his mother as he obviously couldn't decide.

In response, he picked up a pair of Imari vases and started to juggle with them. I was getting really mad at this stage. So I said that I had two boys and wouldn't care for them harassing a local shopkeeper as I am sure his mother wouldn't. He took his time putting them back and sauntered out of the shop. I immediately locked up and put the closed sign on the door. I went to find Keith saying he or one of the boys must stick around in earshot, more especially on a Saturday.

THAT WAS the start of feeling more vulnerable. I had helped run and manage the shop for 33 years. I had had enough when the television programmes kept giving out "that brown furniture wasn't selling". We were also doing quite a few fairs then for that's where the people were. Several of the shops here, for various reasons, had closed so the place was not quite the draw that it was. The dealers were more likely to visit the larger fairs where they could buy from several dealers in one trip.

. . .

WE TRIED the shop as a small centre at one time which worked quite well at first. Then a couple of local guys decided to upset the apple cart by bringing in repro items which was a no-no. We had to ask them to leave.

Eventually things got so quiet and so many other shops had closed that talking to a friend in the business resulted in him coming up to see what he could buy. In the end we did a deal for the majority of the stock in order to close down straightaway. I was relieved. It saved having a sale and facing people and all the hanging around. I had done my stint. Of course I still helped at the Antique Fairs but they were only one-day events.

CHAPTER 10

OUR BOYS

By this time the boys had grown up. Andrew had got married to lovely Heidi. They later presented us with an adorable baby girl called Jasmine.

After four years, delightful Hannah came along and then playful Aaron. What a lovely time we had with them all.

About the same time Andrew married, Nigel moved in with his girlfriend in Kings Lynn. He was studying to become an architect. He managed it after working and studying part time at Greenwich University, and did very well to keep going. He had a deep recession to contend with too. He ended up staying in London and eventually bought a place there.

ANDREW BECAME a manager at a local Co-op then later at a pet, garden and hardware shop which he brought out of the red. He finally had his own shop selling a large range of decorative and antique items as well as painted furniture which became the vogue, the latter by his capable partner, Dawn.

Andrew's and Heidi's three lovely children grew up into wonderful, well-adjusted adults.

Jasmine worked for Aldiss in the Furniture Dept as did Heidi. She later met Jake and gave birth to dear William who is now six. He has become a real joy.

Hannah went to University and finally became a special needs teacher where she met Matthew. They have been married seven years now.

Aaron has his own plumbing business

and his partner, Emily, runs a garden service. They have just bought their own house which they are doing up.

Andrew was always more interested in our business. He took to collecting all sorts of things as a youngster. Old keys were a great favourite which he hung on a board in his room. Copper and brass items, and other quirky things also took his fancy.

NIGEL DELVED in all sorts of things such as magic, puppets, skateboarding, tennis and later, making Dr Who and Star Trek models and various things such as the "time machine". He also learned to play all types of guitars quite beautifully.

In the future, for a few days once a year we would meet up with Nigel who became an architect, living and working in London. We did try to take Sundays off at times to explore the coast taking a picnic or buying fish and chips supper.

When he bought his London house, he turned the garden into a tropical paradise, opening it for the Yellow Gardening

Scheme and the Red Cross for many years, and collecting quite a lot for charity. We helped sometimes with these. It was fun meeting the people, collecting the money and dishing out the tea and cakes.

CHAPTER 11

MY FRIENDS

I DID MAKE SOME GOOD FRIENDS, SUCH AS Nancy and Saul Harris who took us under their wing when we arrived in Swaffham. Nancy was a founder member of the conservation group, and was especially keen to see what we did with the house. She had always been very supportive of me and the boys. We became good friends with a shared love of flowers and gardening. She taught me a lot.

Nancy and Saul were wonderful to the boys too, taking them out so we didn't have to worry about them. They became surrogate grandparents as our parents were so far away. Their own son lived in America so they didn't see a lot of him.

Nancy also introduced me to others who became firm friends such as Mrs Stratton, Pauline Coe and her lovely family, and Queenie Crisp. I also became friends with Queenie's daughter, Ros, who lives in Canada. I met Win through the local Art group which I was encouraged to join and where I did have some success as I won a few prizes for my paintings. I was inscribed on the cup twice when my art was chosen as the top painting of our exhibitions.

Her husband David used to take us swimming to the club in Kings Lynn 9-10pm on a Wednesday evening.

MARGARET SCHER BEFRIENDED me after her husband died suddenly. We would share afternoon tea many times at her flat above Barclays Bank. One day she died in mysterious circumstances when I was away working.

The little room was converted into my

sewing room where I did my art. It was also my little bit of sanctuary.

Fig. 12. My sewing room where I did my art work

I also shared many a lovely tea party with Mavis Lee. We would talk about every subject under the sun. Her husband used to buy little boxes for her as presents. She found several squirrelled away in a drawer after he had gone. We still phone each other now that she has moved to Wiltshire to be nearer her son.

Lots of others have been important mainstay in my life even if it was just to pass the time of day with. Dr Smith, who used live in our house before two others, dropped by one early evening not long after we arrived to introduce himself and his family. He believed that in the "junk room" at the back of the house he found his old unstrung viola which he duly tucked under his arm and went away with.

The boys played with the Smiths' children and Dr David Langman's children. Michelle, David's wife, took them to Wells swimming and a picnic one day where Nigel nearly drowned. The tide had come in and so suddenly he found himself out of his depth which caused him to panic. Thankfully some chap nearby rescued him after he had gone under a few times. He could swim perfectly well but froze. I told him he could have just resorted to doggy paddle which would have kept him afloat. So we learned, and nearly at our cost, how treacherous the tides could be on the North Norfolk Coast.

WE DID LEARN to take many a Sunday off to spend with the boys. Otherwise we were all home, working in our different ways. We explored Norfolk's beaches, woods and stately homes such as Brancaster, Wells, Holkham and Holme next the Sea.

We also visited Thetford Woods and Sandringham as well as Houghton, Holkham, Ickburg, Felbrigg and our favourite, Blickling Hall.

On certain days at the latter, we were allowed to pick a basket of apples to take home.

OF COURSE, friends and family would come to visit. My sister Vanessa (Nessa) would often come with her family. Keith's sister and her family made it up a few times also. My friend Hazel brought her mother and her little girl, Vanya, too. We took them to Sandringham and Bressingham Steam gardens. Keith's uncle and aunt came one time when we took them to Banham Zoo, Motor Museum and Gardens.

WHEN NIGEL WAS STUDYING to become an architect he was based at Banham Zoo for a while and designed the penguin pool, amongst other attractions.

My parents came to marvel at what we were undertaking. I remember one time when Mum had travelled on her own to spend a week's holiday with us. She was so cross when Dad phoned up after a few days to see if Keith would meet him off the train for a long weekend.

Still we had managed to visit Lynn and Norwich for shopping and to see the sights which she enjoyed. It was around the time of my birthday so we took them to Sheringham where I spied some greatly reduced gardening chairs so we all ended up carrying one each up the steep hill.

My second brother came with his wife and children for a long weekend when we took them to Holkham beach. Adam wasn't happy. It turned out he had an abscess on his tooth, poor chap. My sister kicked up a fuss as she was hoping to come too. I said I couldn't cope with them all.

MY YOUNG BROTHER and his wife also stayed many times on their way over to France from Bermuda. We enjoyed exploring with them too. Keith's brother brought his wife and son, Oliver, from his first marriage. It was the hottest day of the year when Keith decided to cook a barbecue.

I seemed to cook in the oven and make salads a lot, which was just as well, because most of Keith's cooking were burnt offerings or in cinders until Nigel and his current lady turned up to take over. All these were memorable days and many more.

. . .

57

THERE WERE several known characters when we came. Most notable amongst them was Reggie Drake — a dapper little man with twinkling eyes. He was a historian as well as a good artist portraying the quirks of the town and the countryside, as was Ben Ripper, the local barber and painter who always had lots of stories to tell.

Then there was the very talented Harry Carter. He was the local art teacher at Hammonds. Some of his work is in the local museum where there is a room dedicated to him. He made the town's Pedlar sign as he did for many towns and villages. He is descended from Howard Carter of Tutankhamen.

Fig. 13. My coloured pencil drawing of Tutankhamen

Howard Carter of Tutankhamen lived in Swaffham as well as some of his relatives.

CHAPTER 12

BRUMAS AND TOMPEY

I ALMOST FORGOT TO MENTION BRUMAS, OUR Old English Sheepdog. How could I forget him? He was loveable but had a mind of his own. He would get very cross if we left him too long, and sit with his head on the step leading to the boiler room and scullery, with his bottom to us as if to say, 'that's what I think of you!'

Although he grew quite large from the dear little bear he was, he was quite gentle and careful. When Keith had done a house clearance spreading the stuff all over the kitchen floor, he would step amongst them, sniffing them all. The amazing thing was he never broke anything.

We used to walk him over the camping land where we trained him to do his "loos" in the hedges, so as not to litter the walking spots. The cows in the next field took a great deal of interest in him as he did in them.

THE ONLY TIME I ever knew him to take anything and eat off the table was when I bought a loaf cake from the Women's Institute. It was then we knew he had a problem. We took him to the vet who sent him to the Veterinary Hospital in Kings Lynn. They discovered an enzyme problem which was sending his food straight through him. He wasn't getting any benefit or nutrition. They recommended special powders and tablets (which he often left) to put into his food.

On talking to Alan Cole one day, he recommended something called "paunch" which is the lining of a cow's stomach with all its munching. Nigel or I would go to the slaughter house on the corner of Cley Road to buy the stuff.

What a smell and so difficult to cut up. It would blunt the knife in seconds. Yet it worked, and Brumas soon put weight back on. His fur was healthier-looking and he was more like his old playful self. It took a while and we dared not give up on the "paunch". However, we were very thankful when a new product came on the market which was in a condensed block form and this could be bought and cut it up easily without the horrendous smell and the gut-wrenching look of the basic stuff.

He was only three years old when this happened. He lived to a grand old age of thirteen which was deemed a good age for a large dog. We still tread over him on that step at times and often smell his damp fur on rainy days.

Fig. 14. Brumas and Tompey, the parrot

Of course I must mention Tompey, the African grey parrot. A few different ones appeared before him. He was stuck in the corner near me in the first floor sitting room, screeching and carrying on in my ear. Either that goes or I do!

After placing him round the drawing room which wasn't ideal, he ended up in the back hallway passage near the kitchen door. There was always someone passing through and we were always calling to each other. So he learned to talk in all our voices causing quite a stir and mix up until we recognised it was him.

We had him for a number of years until he fell ill. Someone may have fed something at Andrew's wedding weekend or something got in his food from the pet shop because it appeared in the autopsy that he had a growth. His death was horrible. It was the first time I had ever heard the "death rattle", one not to be listened to again. He was supposed to outlive us. He was quite a character and I missed him.

CHAPTER 13

THE GARDEN

THE GARDEN WAS QUITE A SANCTUARY, EVEN in the early days when it was just bare bones.

When the heating was being put in and every floorboard seemed to be up, I was able to sit out there planning the kitchen as well as other things due to the good weather in March and April.

When the spring and summer got going, I would visit the Women's Institute stall for plants. I bought mostly flowering shrubs with as many evergreens as I could. I also got cuttings from Mum and Dad's garden, especially the lilac that grew there which came from a cutting where Dad grew up in

Coventry. It grew well in all places and is now at least 10-foot high in our garden and flowers well most years.

Fig. 15. A pen and ink sketch of the garden in its original state

Friends gave me cuttings and often brought plants when they came to stay. I soon learned that some plants did really well and others often just keeled over and died.

I planted lots of roses. These were mixed into the borders and grown on the walls. I did find that having a walled garden was a mixed blessing as the plants didn't really like being up against them, especially having a large weeping ash taking up a lot of light, water and nutrients. I realised, after reading Alan Bloom's book (of Bressingham Gardens fame) that he had the same difficulty about creating island beds.

Plants veered away from the wall for air and light, so he created the island beds where the plants stood up as proud as peacocks and could be seen in all their beauty.

I also liked the wild flowers such as primroses, cowslips, foxgloves and hollyhocks which grew well at first but later the soil became too rich. Mind you, I had lots of stuff in pots as Keith was always threatening to move house again.

*Fig. 16. Painting of topiary under the ash tree planted
by me but cut into a bird shape by Keith*

That was my birthday present solved for many years. The more plants, as I could never resist, the more pots I needed.

My Mother's Day in later years was always spent with Andrew taking me to the Thetford Garden Centre, where we enjoyed a lovely meal and a good look around before he treated me to a few plants that I had spotted. They all flourished.

I also belonged to the Royal Horticultural Society (RHS) and would attend London shows held in their hall there, and of course, the Chelsea Flower Show and the Hampton Court Palace one. I went with Hazel whom I stayed with, so we could enjoy the few days together, seeing Nigel for a day, often at Kew where he was a member.

I stayed with Nigel for a night or two to enjoy time with him and to break up the journey, especially in the latter days when Hazel had moved to Bucks.

I VIVIDLY REMEMBER one day in the middle years after staying with Nigel, having visited the London RHS show, before making my way to Victoria Coach Station to catch the coach back to Swaffham.

I had bought a camellia, a special bi-coloured one, which I had managed to put in my small, neat overnight trolley, so early only the top leaves were poking out.

I went to board the Swaffham coach but the driver said, 'You can't come on here with that! It will have to go in the hold,' The earth would have been upset and gone all over the place. I'd brought back many a plant this way in my little bag tucked neatly between me without interfering with another passenger.

He said he couldn't let me on as it could endanger other passengers. I said, 'Could I ask the others if they minded?' but he wouldn't allow me on. There were just a few leaves poking out at the top— no prickles, flowers, pollen, nothing to harm anyone.

However, he said to get a box or something to put it in to go in the hold. *Well, where was I going to find that?* I did ask all the shops there but no joy.

Then I saw the loo attendants changing the bins with bin liners. After my explanation, they gave me two. I went to make my way over to the coach but when the driver saw me he drove off. I was stunned and shocked. Unbeknown to me, a friend, Mavis was on the coach. She did shout out to the driver that she knew I wanted to board the coach as I lived in her town, to which he replied 'She's not getting on here!'

I went to see various authorities at the station but they were not very helpful. It seemed the Norwich and even Cambridge coaches were full and could not give me a refund, and still I had to apply for that separately.

What to do? I was shaking and very upset by now. I phoned Nigel who said, 'You'd better come back here.' It was evening.

He was going up the road with a friend Craig from University for dinner. He included me which did help to cheer me up. They were both so kind.

I had thought I would leave my plant with Nigel but he is into exotic gardening. As I was travelling back by train, there really was no need. After all, when Chelsea Flower Show was running, people carried all sorts by public transport, even mini trees!

The ticket officer at Kings Cross was most sympathetic when he heard my story and let me have a cheap train ticket.

Keith picked me up from Downham Market Station when I related my tale of woe yet again. After winding down a little, I got to the relevant coach customer services to explain what had happened and that I wanted a refund. They said I had to put it in writing, which I did. After a long wait they refunded my fare but I had to asked for my train fare too due to the unexpected extra cost. They finally did send it.

I also phoned the RHS to tell them how I'd been treated but there was little joy there. I thought they should take it up with the coach people on my behalf and all the many visitors to their shows who would take plants back and had done that for many years after visiting them.

For many years, it put me off travelling by coach — a great shame for in the early years it was such a great service. It took about three hours to travel from Swaffham to London with a stop. The boys and I would often go for the day to take in the museums, Hamleys and other places, ending often at the RHS halls in a day.

Thankful that I had many happy memories before that particular scenario, I never brought plants back again.

Fig. 17. The coach, plant and me

CHAPTER 14

BIRDS

BECAUSE OF ALL THE SHRUBS AND SMALL trees, the walled garden became a haven for birds.

We had a blackbird family and the cheeky, bossy robin as well as the wren, blue tits and coal tits. A pair of hedge sparrows crept around cleaning up after the others had fed. The wood pigeons were good at that too, but oh, what a mess they made. They also trampled on my smaller plants.

One of my favourites were the beautiful chaffinches. One year they nested in the trellis where we could see their babies which was a delight, though, I am not sure how many survived.

Keith craved to have goldfinches but learned you had to put out niger seeds. We waited months for them to come and they did, though they preferred the sunflower hearts. They all did.

We had flocks now. The green finches were in abundance but they are bossy, aggressive birds. I don't care for them much.

We were blessed with a rare treat of a couple of fieldfares and a delightful goldcrest on top of the yew tree "totem pole" I was trying to develop.

The jackdaws were a pain so I would shoo them off as much as possible. They made their long nests in the chimneys causing lots of problems and damage.

The doves were lovely. We had a pair but they nested in the rainwater hoppers causing the gutters to overflow. Keith had to devise a way of stopping them by putting chicken wire, the spiky side up, to deter them. There was also that incessant cooing.

OH! I do remember one time when opening the shop one Saturday morning when I heard a commotion inside. What was it? I discovered a jackdaw flying around so I shut the door quick.

A chap knocked at the door waiting to come in but I explained the delay. He said he would get it for me but I was worried about the damage it would do. I thanked him, said my husband would deal with it and asked if could he come back in half an hour.

Keith got a towel and went in and soon came back with it. I went in to see to damage but amazingly only one glass broken — just lots of droppings everywhere. We opened up the shop.

The chap was waiting outside and as amazed as me that not more damage was done. The jackdaw had obviously come down the chimney.

We did also used to have the beautiful speckled thrush who could be heard tapping the snails on the patio to get at the food inside; very rare these days. We did have the pleasure one time of the nightingale singing at the top of the weeping ash tree. Keith also spotted a tree creeper but I never saw it.

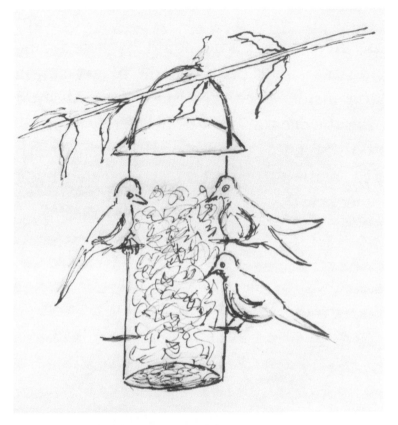

*Fig. 18. The birds on the feeder in the garden outside
the kitchen window*

CHAPTER 15

RESTORATION

AFTER THOSE INITIAL YEARS, KEITH DID much of the work on the house restoring, puttying, painting and so on. In the early years, we had scaffolding erected over the whole front of the house. He had replaced the rotting wood, and restored and painted the dormer windows and the first floor ones.

When the Narford Scaffolding people came to take it down they were so impressed with his work, they gave him some money back, saying, 'take your wife out for dinner on us all... you deserve it!' What a lovely gesture, and so very appreciated.

He has kept this house in pretty good

order over the years which is such an asset to this town. Fortunately, a lot of the people have commended him and shown him the respect he deserves.

It's no mean feat to take on one of these listed buildings. They cost a lot of money, time and effort for all who live in them. We should be thankful that people take them on as they are saved for the nation. For all the work, this house has been lovely to live and work in, as it's so light, airy and such a friendly place to be in.

Work is ongoing as with these houses, but who knows where the next years will take us as Keith is in his 80th year and I am approaching mine.

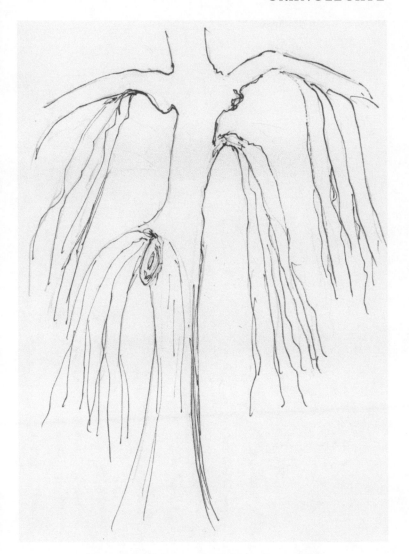

Fig. 19. The weeping ash tree in the garden

LIST OF PLATES

All illustrations and photographs by R D Buckie. Cover illustration: Swaffham Pedlar sign by Nigel Buckie, Cranglegate and King Tut by R D Buckie.

Fig. 1. Cranglegate. Pencil and watercolour on paper.
Fig. 2. Bed picture. Pen and ink on paper.
Fig. 3. Front door of Cranglegate. Pen and Ink on paper
Fig. 4. The boxes. Pen and ink on paper.
Fig. 5. The Main Gates. Pen and ink on paper.
Fig. 6. Me in my black coat. Pen and ink on paper.

Fig. 6a. Andrew as an eagle. Colour photograph.

Fig. 6b. Nigel as a the rear of a pantomime horse. Colour photograph.

Fig. 7. Smouldering logs. Pen and ink on paper.

Fig. 8. Me holding a broom in the hallway. Pen and ink on paper.

Fig. 9. My countryside stews. Watercolour pencils on paper.

Fig. 10. Vegetables on our kitchen table. Pastel on paper. First Prize by Edna Bison.

Fig. 11. Picture of chair and us playing games. Pen and ink on paper.

Fig. 12. My sewing room where I did my art. Pastel on paper.

Fig. 13. Tutankhamen. Coloured pencils on watercolour paper.

Fig. 14. Brumas and Tompey, the parrot. Pen and ink on paper.

Fig. 15. Garden in its original state. Pen and ink on paper.

Fig. 16. Topiary under the Ash tree. Pastel on paper.

Fig. 17. The coach, plant and me. Pen and ink on paper.

Fig. 18. Birds on the feeder. Pen and ink on paper.

Fig. 19. The weeping ash tree in the garden. Pen and ink on paper.

BEFORE YOU GO

The book you are holding in your hand is the result of my dream to be an author. I hope you enjoyed it as much as I enjoyed writing it. As you probably suspected, it takes weeks, months or years to write a book. It exists through dedication, passion and love. Reviews help readers discover authors. Please take *less than a minute* to write me a review on Goodreads or a major online retailer. A big thank you. *Rosalind*

ABOUT THE AUTHOR

Rosalind Buckie was born in Somerset, England, and grew up in Middlesex. One in a family of five, she grew up studying dressmaking and haute couture, spending time in the fashion industry before having a family and moving to the wilds of Norfolk. Here, she and her husband renovated a 17th century listed building where they ran an antique shop for 33 years.

ACKNOWLEDGMENTS

I WOULD LIKE TO thank my son Nigel for all his help, Ivy for editorial work and my publisher, Leopard Print, London and listed building listing description for the reference.

To all of you, my special thanks.